PORSCHE

A celebration of an iconic marque

Mason Crest

Contents

Mason Crest
450 Parkway Drive, Suite D
Broomall, PA 19008
www.masoncrest.com

©2016 by Mason Crest, an imprint of National Highlights, Inc.

Printed and bound in the United States of America.

10 9 8 7 6 5 4 3 2 1

Cataloging-in-Publication Data on file with the Library of Congress.

Series ISBN: 978-1-4222-3275-0
Hardback ISBN: 978-1-4222-3281-1
ebook ISBN: 978-1-4222-8519-0

Written by: Jed Paine

Images courtesy of Magic Car Pics, Corbis and Shutterstock

Introduction

"I couldn't find the sports car of my dreams, so I built it myself."

Ferdinand Porsche

Few car manufacturers can boast such a rich history clearly demonstrating the evolutionary path of their success. For Porsche, they are able to claim the title of being the largest sports car producer in the world, possess an enviable sporting heritage, *and* are the creator of one of automotive history's most iconic cars: the legendary 911.

This publication explores the foundation of the company, delves into the history of Porsche and their contribution to Germany's war effort during the Second World War, and uncovers their brief foray into the field of agricultural vehicles.

Porsche have long since maintained the philosophy that technology in their production vehicles derives from competition models, an ethos that is evident by their use of turbocharged engines, kinetic energy recovery systems (KERS), and Porsche Doppelkupplung (PDK) transmission, to name but a few. Excelling at endurance racing, hillclimb events, and rallying has put Porsche in good stead to develop cars that offer a powerful and thrilling drive.

From the 356 to the 918 Spyder, Porsche have constantly looked for innovative ideas and technology to be leaders in their field and secure their future.

■ **ABOVE: Dr. Ferdinand Porsche in 1940.**

■ **OPPOSITE: Adolf Hitler examines the first Beetle, designed by Ferdinand Porsche who is standing by the car.**

■ **RIGHT: A Porsche 911 Turbo races in the V Historic Rally in Avila, Spain.**

Foundation and
Early History

In 1931 Ferdinand Porsche founded his design consultancy company: Dr. Ing. h. c. F. Porsche GmbH. The Porsche Engineering Office, based in Stuttgart, was established to provide a design service for various means of transportation including airplanes, trains, boats, and, of course, motor vehicles. The first project arrived from the Wanderer Company – to design a 1.7-liter six-cylinder 35 bhp engine. As Dr. Porsche did not want the

Wanderer contract to appear as the first, and to avoid any doubts that he lacked experience in this field, he labeled it the Porsche Type 7 and continued to number the subsequent cars in consecutive order. This explains why there aren't any early designed models that are labeled one to six. Wanderer soon returned with more business, and requested a more powerful engine: the result was a 2.0-liter six-cylinder 40 bhp engine. In the

August of 1931, Ferdinand Porsche registered a patent for the torsion bar suspension – a development that would be used internationally for several decades and is considered a significant achievement in automotive history.

In 1932, the Auto Union Company (which would later become the present-day Audi) took over the car division of Wanderer in a merger between Horch, Audi, and DKW. Impressed by the

Type 7 designed by Porsche, the Auto Union Company later asked him and his team to design a new Grand Prix car. Adolf Hitler had announced two new programs: the People's Car, which would later become the Volkswagen Beetle, and a state-sponsored motor racing program, which required a German firm to develop cars in the new 1653-lb formula.

They created the 16-cylinder 1653-lb Auto Union P racing car, which set three world records in 1934 and was one of the most successful racing cars of the inter-war era. The mid-engined configuration pioneered the trend for modern racing cars and is

still used in Formula One to the present day.

Porsche also designed a sleek-looking coupe named the Type 8: it boasted an eight-cylinder 3.25-liter engine and Ferdinand Porsche used it for many years for his own personal use.

The Auto Union project provided Porsche with an exciting opportunity, but since money was required to keep the company afloat they became heavily involved in the design of military vehicles during the lead up to the Second World War, resulting in the creation of the Kübelwagen and the Schwimmwagen. Translated as "bucket car," the Volkswagen

Kübelwagen was an inexpensive lightweight military transport vehicle based on the Beetle that was first created in 1938. Experienced military coachbuilder, Trutz, constructed the bodywork, and by November 1938 developmental testing of the first vehicle, known as the Type 62, commenced. The Kübelwagen handled rough terrain surprisingly well, despite its lack of four-wheel drive capabilities, and overall it was well received by military commanders who requested only two changes: to reduce its lowest speed from 5 mph to 2.5 mph to adjust to the pace of marching soldiers, and to further improve its off-road performance.

The Type 82 was subsequently launched, incorporating the required changes. Extensive testing on snow and ice was necessary to ensure it would be able to cope with the European winters. The smooth flat underbody enabled the vehicle to steadily propel itself along when the wheels sank into snow, mud, or sand.

The VW Type 128 and 166 Schwimmwagen was an amphibious four-wheel drive off-roader, which utilized the engine and mechanicals of the Type 86 Kübelwagen.

■ ABOVE: A 1943 Volkswagen Schwimmwagen.

■ RIGHT: A Cisitalia race car designed by Ferdinand Porsche.

However, the flat floorpan chassis that worked effectively for the Kübelwagen was unsuitable for movement through water, leading to some initial issues with the prototype (Type 128). The successful Type 166 went on to be one of the most numerous mass-produced amphibious vehicles with more than 14,265 manufactured.

During the five and a half years of war, the company had no choice but to work for their country – designing and building whatever vehicles were required. Their loyalty to their country led them to submit designs for heavy tanks, including the Elefant tank destroyer and the Panzer VIII Maus super-heavy tank.

In November 1945, Professor Ferdinand Porsche was asked to redesign the Volkswagen Beetle in a "more French" style. However, disagreements between the French government and the car manufacturing firm led by Jean Pierre Peugeot meant the project never made it off the ground.

The French authorities arrested Professor Ferdinand Porsche, his son Ferry, and the company lawyer (who was also Ferdinand's son-in-law) Anton Piëch on December 15, 1945. Ferry was released soon after, his family paying the bail of 500,000 francs that was requested. He moved to Austria where he managed the company with his elder sister Louisa. They set to work on two new automobiles; they constructed a racing car for the Cisitalia racing team and designed their own car: the Porsche 356. Meanwhile, Ferdinand was taken to a prison in Dijon; he remained there for 22 months in squalid conditions and his health deteriorated. It was not until 1947, at the age of 73, that he was released, along with Anton Piëch, when Ferry had gathered the

funds to pay the bail. The Porsche family returned to Stuttgart in 1949 in order to accommodate the production of the popular 356, and in November 1950 Ferdinand Porsche made his last visit to the Wolfsburg Volkswagen factory. The factory was full of activity and Ferdinand is said to have been delighted with the massive production of the Beetle that he had designed. The family set about creating an emblem that would represent the company and become a worldwide-recognized crest.

Since 1952 all Porsche cars have been branded with the iconic logo on the bonnet. Early models sported a neat silver script announcing the Porsche name. Professor Ferdinand

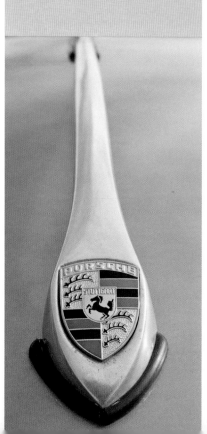

■ **RIGHT:** Rows of completed Volkswagen Beetles sit outside the Volkswagen factory in Wolfsburg.

■ **BELOW:** A Porsche 356A proudly displaying the Porsche logo.

Porsche and his son Ferry set about creating a company emblem that would exude a powerful image – an icon that proudly acknowledged its Stuttgart roots. Countless drafts were produced before the final crest was designed. The Porsche shield is based on the coat of arms of the Free People's State of Württemberg (Weimar-era Württemberg coat of arms), featuring antlers and the

black and red stripes. The arms of Stuttgart are placed at the center, depicting a black horse "rampant" in reference to the city's beginnings as a stud farm. The appearance of the horse also represents power and forward motion. The 356 was the first car to wear the Porsche crest, first appearing on the center of the steering wheel and later on the bonnet. Unfortunately it was

something that Ferdinand Porsche didn't get to see before his death on January 30, 1951, aged 75.

Following his father's death, Ferry drove the company on. A massive contract with Volkswagen benefited Porsche greatly: for every Beetle sold, Porsche would receive a share of the profits. Demand for the 356 was still high, and despite the initial planned production of

only 1,500 units, Porsche went on to build more than 78,000 356s over the next 17 years. Their involvement in racing also increased, following a victory at 24 Hours of Le Mans in 1951.

It was the start of a new era in which Porsche would promote and enhance their brand, securing a respected status among car manufacturers and enthusiasts alike.

Coming of Age

■ **ABOVE: The Porsche Standard Star 219.**

In 1934 Ferdinand Porsche developed the first Porsche diesel motor for the Porsche tractor. It may come as a surprise that he briefly dabbled in the field of agricultural vehicles during the company's early years. He produced three prototype tractors that year that included hydraulic coupling between engine and transmission. Although development of an air-cooled diesel engine was underway it was not yet ready for production, so the three prototypes all featured petrol engines.

In 1937 there was an official order from the German government to develop a "Volks-Tractor," so while developing the "people's car," Professor Ferdinand Porsche was also designing the "people's tractor."

Numerous tests were carried out

on the air-cooled diesel engine and by the early 1950s four basic models had been designed in one-, two-, three-, and four-cylinder versions with a power output ranging from 14-44 bhp. A four-wheel drive tractor was also on the drawing board as early as 1946. Following the end of the Second World War, Porsche signed licensing agreements with Allgaier GmbH and Hofherr Schrantz, allowing them to use their modern and uniquely designed engine. The result was the creation of the Allgaier – System Porsche and the Hofherr Schrantz – System Porsche.

In 1959 Mannesmann AG bought the license for the Porsche diesel engine and the Allgaier tractor design and went on to produce over 125,000 Porsche-Diesel tractors.

Qualität durch Erfahrung — das war bei der Entwicklung des Typs 911 der Grundsatz der Porsche-Konstrukteure.

Ein exklusiver in allen Geschwindigkeitsbereichen ideal abgestufter Reisewagen verwandelt sich, zügig gefahren, in ein sportliches Coupé europäischer Elite.

Nicht Transport oder Repräsentation, sondern das beglückende Gefühl — Fahren um des Fahrens willen — begründet die alte Porsche-Formel „Fahren in seiner schönsten Form".

Excellence through experience — the maxim guiding Porsche designers in their work on Type 911.

An exclusive touring car, with its perfectly graduated speed ranges, it converts into a sporting coupé of the European elite.

The traditional Porsche slogan "Driving at its finest" expresses not simply the quality of movement or mechanism, but the joy of driving for its own sake.

La qualité grâce à l'expérience — tel fut le principe fondamental des usines Porsche lors de l'étude du type 911.

Une voiture de tourisme exceptionnelle, idéale et bien adaptée à tous les régimes, se transformant, lorsqu'elle est conduite rapidement, en un coupé sportif de standing européen.

Ce n'est pas son côté utilitaire ni son bel aspect, mais la sensation merveilleuse éprouvée à «conduire pour la joie de conduire» qui a créé le vieux slogan de Porsche: «Joie de conduire dans sa plus belle expression».

The last Porsche tractors were built in 1963: a date that signaled the start of a new era in the history of their road production cars.

In 1963 a car designed by Ferry's eldest son, Ferdinand Alexander "Butzi" Porsche, made its debut at the Frankfurt Motor Show. It was the start of an epic journey for one of automotive history's most renowned vehicles: the 911. For five decades it has been the most significant development within the Porsche brand, becoming an iconic sports car that has continued to raise the benchmark for performance and desirability in the automotive industry. Few companies can boast such a remarkable vehicle that has continued to evolve throughout its lifetime.

■ ABOVE: An early 911 brochure from 1965.

Drawings of the car can be traced back as far as 1959 as it was developed to replace the 356 as a more superior model in terms of style, performance, and comfort. It was originally named the 901, but French manufacturer Peugeot objected to the use of a three-number name that used a zero in the middle (in France they had exclusive rights to car names using this formula). From that point on it was publicly known as the 911. The first examples of the car went on sale in the US with a retail price of $6,500.

The 911 is the most developed sports car in history, and in its early years Porsche were not afraid to break the rules in order to create their masterpiece. Despite the belief that the engine should be positioned in front of the rear axle, Porsche placed its flat-six air-cooled engine close to the rear taillights.

The distinctive shape of the 911 is instantly recognizable and was based on the general shape of the 356; its arched body and supreme build quality have been a tribute to German engineering. Although reminiscent of the 356, the 911 body was more aerodynamic than its predecessor. In terms of performance the 911 gave a thrilling ride; the early cars of 1963 were able to offer an engaging relationship with the driver. Impressive acceleration coupled with challenging handling characteristics gave the 911 an edge over its rivals. It was a powerful car that demanded respect. The flat-six air-cooled engine offered breathtaking performance, delivering 130 bhp and a top speed of 130 mph. Turbo editions of the 911 featured wide wheel arches and a large rear spoiler (often referred to as the ducktail). The powerful engine could produce 260 bhp and the cars were known for their exhilarating performance.

The Porsche 911 has already celebrated its 50th anniversary and still remains one of the world's leading sports cars. Their enduring formula for success is a testament to Porsche's commitment to developing and improving the model. It's no secret that the 911 has a strong racing heritage and Porsche's involvement in motorsport has influenced the car's evolution, continuously testing the technology developed for track and applying it to their production cars. Throughout its extensive lifetime the 911 has enjoyed success in racing, rallying, and other automotive competitions. Naturally aspirated 911 Carrera RSRs had regular victories during the 1970s at major world championship sports car races including the Nürburgring, Sebring, Daytona, and Targa Florio.

More than 50 years on, the legacy of the 911 continues – offering an iconic body style, versatile and exhilarating performance, all to the tune of Porsche's unique engine sound.

■ **ABOVE: A Porsche 911 (964) Turbo.**

■ **OPPOSITE: A Porsche Carrera RSR at the Nürburgring in 1973.**

356

The 356 was the first production automobile to bear the Porsche name, and more than 78,000 cars were sold during its 17 years in production. Despite the shattered industrial infrastructure that Germany was experiencing, the post-war creation established an excellent reputation for the company. They had relocated to a former sawmill at Gmünd in Austria where they had set to work on designing the prototype 356. It relied heavily on mechanicals from Volkswagen (the Beetle in particular) and the design initially featured a tubular spaceframe chassis, aluminum body, and a mid-mounted 1131 cc engine capable of producing 35 bhp. Before the prototype was completed they had already finalized plans for a convertible and hardtop version, which would feature a simple box-section chassis, and placement of the gearbox and engine would change to make the new 356 a rear-engined car. Only 50 Gmünd models were built and each one was completed to owner specification, making each individual vehicle unique. Orders for the 356 kept arriving and the basic assembly facilities at the former sawmill were no longer adequate; it was time for Porsche to return to Stuttgart.

In 1950 they released their first official Porsche 356 (the Stuttgart model), which had many similarities to its predecessor. Known as the Pre-A, its body was made of steel due to the lack of aluminum welding facilities at the Reutter factory. The Porsche name was neatly positioned in silver script writing on the nose of the car; it wasn't until 1954 that it carried the iconic badge. The Pre-A initially

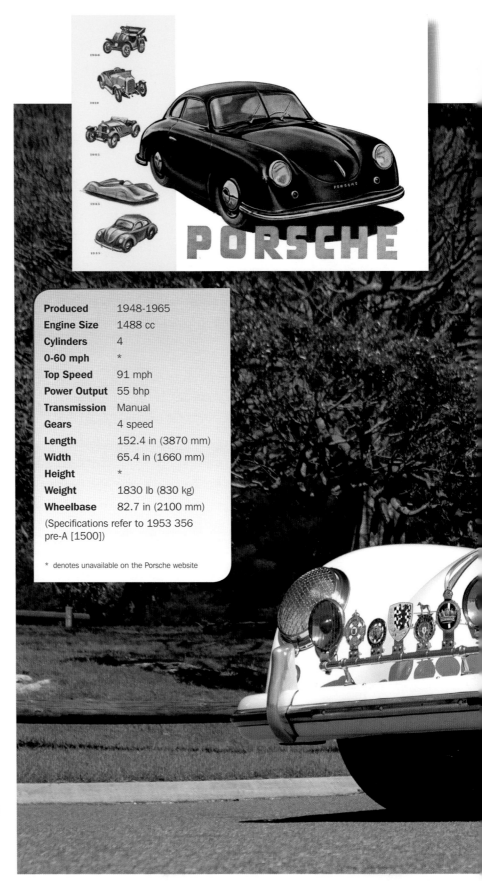

Produced	1948-1965
Engine Size	1488 cc
Cylinders	4
0-60 mph	*
Top Speed	91 mph
Power Output	55 bhp
Transmission	Manual
Gears	4 speed
Length	152.4 in (3870 mm)
Width	65.4 in (1660 mm)
Height	*
Weight	1830 lb (830 kg)
Wheelbase	82.7 in (2100 mm)

(Specifications refer to 1953 356 pre-A [1500])

* denotes unavailable on the Porsche website

featured a compact 1.1-liter engine that produced 40 bhp, but customer demand for more power and improved performance led to a 1.3-liter engine with a displacement of 1286 cc becoming available in 1951. The 356 experienced rapid evolution during its early years in production and by 1954 modifications to the engine resulted

in a worldwide respected sports car. Part of Porsche's success was due to their value of customer feedback and knowledge gained from motorsport developments. They revealed the 356A at the Frankfurt Motor Show in 1955, which featured an increased-capacity engine of 1582 cc. It had improved traction and a new gearbox design, and changes to the cabin made it more sumptuous: padded sun visors, an upholstered dash, and speakers fitted in the footwells all contributed to making the 356A a luxurious car.

911

The 911 is without doubt one of automotive history's most iconic cars and remains the flagship vehicle in the 21st century line-up at Porsche. Having already celebrated its 50th anniversary in production, the 911 has a rich history and is responsible for major evolutionary changes within the Porsche brand. It has been a highly successful model in rallying, endurance racing, and other forms of automotive competition, and can boast distinctive styling and breathtaking performance.

The original 911 was launched at the Frankfurt Motor Show in 1963 and was intended as a more powerful, comfortable replacement to its predecessor – the 356. Featuring a flat-six air-cooled rear-mounted engine, the 911 was capable of achieving a 0-60 performance in 8.5 seconds and could power on to a top speed of 130 mph. Just three years into its production life and the 911 was subject to engine modifications, resulting in the 911S. The 2.0-liter engine was tweaked to produce an additional 30 bhp, thus pushing power output to an impressive 160 bhp and adding a further 6 mph to the maximum speed. The 911S featured five-spoke alloy wheels and an additional rear anti-roll bar. A semi-automatic "Sportomatic" model made its way to the 911 family in 1967. In 1969 Porsche addressed the 911's tendency to over steer by lengthening the wheelbase by 2.24 in (57 mm).

STANDARD EQUIPMENT

Windows
Electric windshield washer system combined with windshield wiper operation
Three-speed windshield wiper
FM suppressed windshield wiper motor
Quarter windows, burglarproof, front and rear
Antiglare interior rear view mirror
Laminated windshield
Rear window ventilation

Lights
Two back-up lights
Infinitely variable instrument illumination
Two fog lamps
Luggage compartment illumination

Signal System
Two super-tone horns
Headlight signal

Instruments
Speedometer with total and trip mileage recorder
Tachometer
Fuel gauge with low level warning light
Oil level gauge
Oil temperature gauge
Oil pressure gauge
Indicator lights for generator, high beam, parking lights,
turn signals, handbrake, fog lamps and heating system
Electric clock with elapsed time indicator

Locks
Both doors equipped with locks operated from inside
as well as outside
Glove compartment with lock
Fuel tank cap operated from car interior
Steering wheel lock combined with ignition lock

Interior
Top and bottom-cushioned antiglare dashboard with wood
panelling in center
Cigarette lighter combined with electrical outlet
Courtesy grip for passenger on door inside
Arm rests designed as door-pulls
Seat belt anchorages
Fasteners for luggage straps

Clothes hanger hook at each door post
Two cushioned sun visors with make-up mirror
Map pocket in each door
Reclining seats
Heater and fresh air vents
Rear seats fold down for extra luggage space -- nonslip
Parcel shelf behind rear seats with nonslip bar
Carpeted floors with shoe-heel protection on driver's side
Slide-in ashtray

Miscellaneous
Tow ring under front of car
Combustion heater
Draftfree ventilation through headlining
Undercoating
Touch-up paint dispenser
7 standard colors and 6 interior combinations to choose from

Produced	1963 to present
Engine Size	1991 cc
Cylinders	6
0-60 mph	8.5 secs
Top Speed	130 mph
Power Output	130 bhp
Transmission	Manual
Gears	5 speed
Length	163.9 in (4163 mm)
Width	63.4 in (1610 mm)
Height	51.9 in (1320 mm)
Weight	2380 lb (1080 kg)
Wheelbase	87 in (2211 mm)

(Specifications refer to 1963
Porsche 911)

Ten years after its premiere in 1963, Porsche unveiled the next generation of 911s – the "G" model, remaining in production for 16 years, making it the longest of all the 911 generations. The 911

Carrera RS was introduced in 1973 and to this day is considered to be one of the greatest 911s of all time. The RS suffix stands for Rennsport, meaning Race Sport. The Carrera RS was developed as a production car in order for Porsche to meet requirements of racing classes that specify a minimum number of road cars are built. Compared to the 911S the Carrera RS featured a larger engine, mechanical fuel injection, wider rear wheels, and larger brakes. In order to meet the requirements of the FIA Group 4 class, Porsche were required to build and sell 500 examples of this model, however the Carrera RS proved popular and they went on to sell more than 1,500 units. The "G" series era also marked the arrival of the first 911 Cabriolet and the 911 Turbo (930).

The 911 remained unchanged for a number of years and it was not until 1985 that it underwent some major alterations, signaling the arrival of the real second-generation 911. The 911 Carrera 4 (964) offered a modern and sustainable vehicle that had experienced a number of changes. It featured a completely redesigned chassis with light alloy control arms and coil springs. Cosmetically it was distinctly different: it now featured aerodynamic polyurethane bumpers and an automatically retractable rear spoiler that accentuated the recognizable 911 shape.

Performance-wise the 3600 cc six-cylinder, air-cooled engine could produce 250 bhp, boast 0-60 in 5.7 seconds, and thunder on to a magnificent top speed of 162 mph. The new 911 also held a

multilink suspension, improved the car's ride and handling, making it incredibly agile. For many, the 933 is a significant model: it was the last 911 to feature an air-cooled engine as from 1998 a new water-cooled engine was favored for the 996 generation.

Today the 911 model remains the most popular car in the Porsche line-up. Internally known as the 991 it represents the greatest technical development in the 911's proud history. It is the quintessential

revolutionary feature – a four-wheel drive system. That, coupled with ABS, power steering, and airbags, ensured that the Carrera 4 would be viewed as a serious upgrade to an already iconic vehicle.

Porsche went on to reinvent the 911 for a second time in 1993, and from the onset they were inundated with demand for this revamped model. The 933 generation essentially just experienced a makeover, although the iconic 911 profile still remained. Styled by Tony Hatter under supervision of design chief Harm Lagaay, significant adjustments were made to the front and rear bumper assemblies in order to improve the aerodynamics, and smoother lines and an aggressive stance enabled the car to appear modern without losing its classic design.

It was the first 911 with a predominantly aluminum chassis, which, coupled with an all-new example of Porsche intelligence, offering increased performance yet less consumption. Powered by a 3.4-liter engine that can generate 350 bhp, the 991 can demonstrate a 0-60 sprint in 4.6 seconds for manual models. Those fitted with PDK can achieve 0-60 in 4.4 seconds.

The 911 model has evolved dramatically during its extensive lifetime and remains one of the most desired sports cars in the world.

912

First introduced in 1965, the Porsche 912 was quickly manufactured as a contingency sales plan, as there had been some speculation over whether the 911 model would sell as many units as the company had planned. The high production costs of the 911 meant that there had to be a high price tag attached to the car, causing it to be less appealing to those with a smaller budget. The 912 was essentially a redesigned, slimmed-down, entry-level version of the 911. The Type 912 was shaped around the classic 911 chassis, with a 1.6-liter four-cylinder pushrod engine that boasted 90 bhp and a top speed of 119 mph. Aside from the mechanical differences to that of the 911, the 912 demonstrated a better weight distribution, superior handling, and a better range; some of the more standard features of the pricier 911 were also removed from the 912 production. These big differences meant that the car was more affordable and initially more popular: for the first few years, the 912 outsold the 911 until Porsche were able to see a rise in sales of the more expensive model.

The 912 was a very attractive vehicle for clients; it looked like a 911 but cost much less to purchase and run. Porsche discontinued the production of the 912's predecessor (the 356) in 1965, paving the way for the production of the 912. Due to its increasing popularity, Porsche manufactured almost 30,000 units of the standard model and nearly 2,500 units of the cabriolet version; the cabriolet (targa top) featured a removable roof and heavy-duty plastic rear window. A more poignant part of the 912's

Produced	1965-1969 and 1976
Engine Size	1582 cc
Cylinders	4
0-60 mph	11.6 secs
Top Speed	119 mph
Power Output	90 bhp
Transmission	Manual
Gears	5 speed
Length	162.8 in (4135 mm)
Width	63 in (1600 mm)
Height	51.9 in (1320 mm)
Weight	2127 lb (965 kg)
Wheelbase	88.7 in (2255 mm)

(Specifications refer to 1965 Porsche 912)

history is that the 100,000th vehicle ever manufactured by Porsche was a 912 Targa that was specially designed for the police force of Baden-Württemberg. It was only in 1969 that the 912 was initially discontinued due to varying factors, both financial and economical, however in 1976 the 912E was reintroduced in North America. The 912E featured an 86 bhp 2.0-liter four-cylinder engine that was again designed to act as an entry-level model once the 914 had been removed from production.

914

The development of the 914 was the result of a collaboration between Porsche and Volkswagen: Porsche had identified that they needed a new entry-level sports car, while Volkswagen needed a replacement for their Karmann Ghia. A deal was struck between the two manufacturers to produce a two-seater, mid-engined roadster powered by a flat-four-cylinder engine in Volkswagen-branded models, and a flat-six-cylinder engine in Porsche models. However, during production it was decided that since the two

models would be sharing the same body, it should be badged by one manufacturer for the North American market. Both versions went on sale with the Porsche badge.

The body was constructed by coachbuilder Karmann while the design was created by Gugelot Design, a German company that had previously expressed an interest in future sports car projects. Numerous drawings were submitted before the final design was chosen. There had been one stipulation made by the two

manufacturers – that it must not resemble any previous Porsche or Volkswagen models. The neat and chiseled design they presented met the criteria; their new approach featured a removable targa roof section and offered a surprising amount of boot space.

The 914 made its debut at the 1969 Frankfurt Automobile Show and had a 1.7-liter four-cylinder air-cooled engine that could generate 80 bhp. However, the 0-60 acceleration of 12.4 seconds, and a top speed of 110 mph, didn't thrust the car to the top of many motoring

Produced	1969-1976
Engine Size	1679 cc
Cylinders	4
0-60 mph	12.4 secs
Top Speed	110 mph
Power Output	80 bhp
Transmission	Manual
Gears	5 speed
Length	159.4 in (4050 mm)
Width	64.9 in (1650 mm)
Height	48.8 in (1240 mm)
Weight	2138 lb (970 kg)
Wheelbase	96.4 in (2450 mm)

(Specifications relate to Porsche 914 1.7)

One of the great frustrations of owning a 2-seater sports car has always been the lack of trunk space. Because most 2-seaters are built with a trunk that accommodates little more than a spare tire.

The Porsche 914 has two ways to beat that problem. One is a 9-cubic-foot trunk in front of the driver, the other is a 7-cubic-foot trunk behind the engine.

That means you can go away on a weekend jaunt, for instance, without borrowing your friend's station wagon. Because the 914 lets you take all the things you need. Suitcases, handbags, groceries, a bushel of clams, whatever.

The same holds true if you're going on a long trip. You can take a pretty friend along, and, in fact, have his and hers trunks.

There are a number of reasons for so much trunk space in our 2-seater.

The first, of course, is the mid-engine placement. It leaves lots of room front and rear. The engine itself is built to save space. It's flat with horizontally opposed cylinders. And being air-cooled it doesn't have a big, bulky radiator to contend with. Even the suspension system is designed to take up less space on the floor of the front luggage compartment.

So if you've been thinking about a 2-seater, think about this: Should you get a 2-seater with a trunk that handles little more than a spare tire?

Or a 914 with a good-sized trunk at both ends?

*Source: Road & Track

You can pack a weekend full of fun into it.

fanatics' wish lists. Speed aside, the 914 was superbly balanced, courtesy of the mid-engined layout, affording it excellent weight distribution. Performance issues were soon addressed and the 914/6 arrived on the market. It featured a carbureted flat-six from the 1969 911T, in addition to the gearbox from the 911, although it was configured for a mid-engine layout. The improved 2.0-liter engine produced 110 bhp and 116 lb/ft of torque at 4,200 rpm. Performance-wise the 914/6 could achieve a far more impressive 8.8 seconds for the 0-60 sprint and could accelerate on to a top speed of 123 mph. The 914/6 variant also offered far more superior handling than the flat-four-engined 914, thanks to a similar suspension and brakes found on the 911.

However, issues with rust and reliability affected the 914/6 sales. Although marketed as a Porsche in the United States, the VW-Porsche branded cars were not suited to either of the manufacturers' usual market. Volkswagen customers were discouraged by the price, which was still out of their reach (despite the creation of the 914 to be destined for the entry-level sports car market), while Porsche clientele regarded it as an inferior model. At the time that it went on sale the 914/6 was only slightly cheaper than the 911T – a car that was regarded

The Porsche 914 gives you more <u>usable</u> luggage space than any other major imported 2-seater.

of Ferdinand Piëch, who wanted to prove the concept. The second was a silver road-registered car that was powered by a detuned 908 race engine capable of generating 260 bhp. The car was presented to Ferry Porsche to mark the celebration of his 60th birthday.

Throughout the course of its production years, the 914 was subject to a number of changes, ranging from minor cosmetic alterations to crash protection features as a result of changing standards. In 1973, Porsche released a modified version of the entry-level 914 that featured a 2.0-liter four-cylinder air-cooled engine capable of producing 100 bhp and a top speed of 116 mph. Externally

the car also featured bumper guards to the front, and one year later had guards added to the rear of the car.

Porsche released a limited-edition run of the 914 series in North America to commemorate their triumph in the Can Am racing series. Two unique color schemes were available on the 1,000 cars that were built. The "Bumblebee" sported black exterior paint coupled with a sunflower yellow trim, while the "Creamsicle" featured a cream body with phoenix red trim, valences, bumper, and Mahle wheels. The 914 SE variants were equipped with dual horns, anti-sway bars, leather-covered steering wheel, and specially designed front spoiler.

as far more superior in terms of performance and styling. Therefore, it was felt that the 914 was simply too expensive for the performance it offered. In 1972 Porsche made the decision to discontinue the 914/6 due to slow sales and rising costs for production.

Two prototype variants of the 914 named 914/8 were built in 1969, featuring a flat-eight racing engine that could produce 310 bhp. The first was built under instruction

930/911 Turbo

Produced	1975-1989
Engine Size	3299 cc
Cylinders	6
0-60 mph	5.3 secs
Top Speed	160 mph
Power Output	300 bhp
Transmission	Manual
Gears	4 speed
Length	169 in (4293 mm)
Width	69.8 in (1773 mm)
Height	51.5 in (1310 mm)
Weight	2961 lb (1343 kg)
Wheelbase	89.4 in (2273 mm)

(Specifications refer to 1978 Porsche
911 Turbo [Type 930])

Porsche introduced the first turbocharged 911 at the Paris Motor Show in 1974. It was the mark of a definitive race-bred sports car – a street-legal version of one of the most successful cars in endurance racing.

Although marketed as the 911 Turbo throughout Europe, it retained its internal type number for North American marketing and was therefore known as the Porsche 930. Porsche initially intended the 930 to be a homologation special edition model in order to qualify for racing, and the distinctive body style with large wheel arches and "whale-tail" spoiler reflected this. Eligibility also relied on Porsche building and selling 400 examples of the model, which it achieved without issues. In fact, demand for the car was so high that during its 14 years in production Porsche sold more than 21,000 cars. Homologation regulations changed, and although

Porsche no longer needed to meet the former requirements the 930 provided the basis for the racing vehicles 934 and 935.

Porsche design engineer Ernst Fuhrmann was responsible for the development of the 930 – he adapted technology from racing and applied it to the road car. The original 930 featured a 3.0-liter flat-six engine with a single KKK (Kuhnle Kopp & Kausch) turbocharger that produced 260 bhp at 5,500 rpm, enabling acceleration from 0-60 in six seconds and a top speed of 155 mph. In order to manage the extra power created it was necessary to revise the suspension and employ a stronger four-speed gearbox in place of the five-speed transmission in standard 911s. The distinctive "whale-tail" spoiler created increased downforce and vented air to the engine. Upgraded wider tires maximized the 930's grip, resulting in more stability. However, although it offered fast performance it was a demanding drive that was far from perfect. Marginal brakes and the rev counter indicates turbo charge boost pressure.

The suspension system, incorporating a special Turbo steering geometry, proves that a sports car need not be synonymous with a hard ride. In this, the ultra low-profile series-50 tyres – specially developed for the Turbo – play a vital part: their width is twice their height and they set totally new standards of safety and road-holding under all conditions, i. e. at speed, cornering braking, and water dispersal. They are fitted to forged alloy rims, 7 inches wide at the front and 8 inches at the back, and are housed under flared wheel arches.

The under stressed braking system, with internally ventilated disc and large, equally well cooled 4-piston calipers, comes straight from the Turbo's racing version, as do the wheel bearings.

After final assembly and checks, every Turbo is subjected to an extended 100 km road test and even more comprehensive inspection programme.

tricky handling caused by its short wheelbase and mid-engine layout lent it to over steer, meaning that the original 930 was a little "rough and ready." Nevertheless, it was a thrilling model. The 930 had also gained popularity on the track too, winning Le Mans on its first outing. The 934 (the racing version of the 930) qualified for the FIA Group 4 competition in 1976, and was swiftly followed by the FIA Group 5 version called the Porsche 935.

In 1978 Porsche raised the bar by making significant upgrades to the 930: the Bosch K-Jetronic fuel injection and KKK turbocharger remained but engine capacity rose to 3.3-liters and, with the addition of the air-to-air intercooler, power output was increased to 300 bhp. On the road those changes translated to an increased top speed of 160 mph and a 0-60 sprint in 5.3 seconds. The 0-100 mph was achieved in an impressive 12.3 seconds, a production car record. The brakes also received an upgrade, with Porsche adding a unit similar to the 917 race car. Externally the 930 experienced only minor changes; the familiar rear spoiler was restyled into what became known as the "tea tray" and repositioned to make way for the newly added intercooler.

The 930 was about more than just raw power and speed; while the standard 911 offered a challenging drive experience, the Turbo took that to the next level, demanding an increased level of respect.

In 1980 the 930 had to be withdrawn from the US and Japanese market due to changing emission regulations. It remained in European markets (under the 911 Turbo name) and in 1983 was offered with a 325 bhp performance option for those wishing to purchase one of the build-to-order models. The package also included a four-pipe exhaust system and additional oil cooler. These editions can be identified by the additional ventilation holes in the rear fenders and remodeled front spoiler.

In 1981 the Flachbau (slantnose) 930 was made available under the special order program. Essentially it was a 911 model featuring a 935-style slanting nose. To achieve the Flachbau model each unit was handcrafted by remodeling the front fenders. It is believed that only 948 of this model were constructed, each one featuring the 330 bhp performance kit as standard.

The 930 was reintroduced in US and Japanese markets in 1986 with targa and cabriolet variants – both proved to be highly popular. In order to comply with emission regulations they were fitted with an emission-controlled engine that could produce 278 bhp.

It was only in its final year of production that Porsche exchanged the four-speed transmission for a five-speed gearbox (called the G50) and a new hydraulic clutch enabled smoother shifting between gears. These additions alone increased the car's desirability. The 1989 model also addressed driver and passenger comfort. The full leather interior, seat heating, and six-way adjustable seats, ensured increased luxury.

924

The Porsche 924 made its first official appearance at La Grande Motte, Camargue in France in 1975. It was well received and went on to be a successful model, selling more than 150,000 units during its time in production. Not only did it save the company from financial trouble, it created a much-needed revenue stream to continue the development of the legendary 911.

The 924 was a two-door 2+2 four-cylinder front-engined, water-cooled coupe that was initially intended to be Volkswagen's leading sports car; during its development it was named Project 425. Following an agreement made between the two companies back in the 1950s, Porsche were to develop a sports car that would work with the VW/Audi in-line four engine. However following the 1973 oil crisis, and a change in Volkswagen's company directors, Project 425 was put on hold before being completely scrapped in favor of a less expensive and more practical Scirocco model. Since Porsche needed a model to replace the 914, they decided to buy the designs back for $40 million and launched the 924 into production at the former NSU factory in Neckarsulm, where Volkswagen would build the cars under Porsche's instruction.

Harm Lagaay, a member of the Porsche styling team, was responsible for the overall wedge-shaped appearance. The bonnet smoothly sloped down, concealing retractable headlamps, while the nose was grille-less. The original version was available with a four-speed manual transmission (sourced from Audi) and in 1977 a three-speed automatic was offered. US models were subject to emission control, resulting in a power output of 95 bhp from the Bosch

Produced	1976-1988
Engine Size	2984 cc
Cylinders	4
0-60 mph	9.9 secs
Top Speed	124 mph
Power Output	125 bhp
Transmission	Manual
Gears	4 speed
Length	169.8 in (4313 mm)
Width	65.9 in (1676 mm)
Height	49.6 in (1260 mm)
Weight	2380 lb (1080 kg)
Wheelbase	94.4 in (2400 mm)

(Specifications relate to 1976 Porsche 924)

K-Jetronic fuel injection engine, while European models generated 125 bhp.

In 1979 a version featuring a five-speed transmission became available. Throughout its production years, the 924 experienced only minor changes. It was rated highly for its styling, fuel economy, and handling, but motoring critics cited that the car delivered a poor performance. However, this changed with the arrival of the 924 Turbo models, bridging the gap between the basic 924 model and the renowned 911.

Porsche engineers had already experienced first-hand the benefit of turbochargers in both race and road car applications and in 1978 introduced the 924 Turbo.

The addition of the KKK K-26 turbocharger (without intercooler) into the engine enhanced power and torque dramatically, generating 170 bhp and 181 lb/ft respectively. The 924 Turbo could sprint from 0-60 in 7.7 seconds and boasted a top speed of 142 mph. In order to improve engine cooling, a NACA duct (a low-drag air inlet) was added in the badge panel of the nose. Left-hand drive models were dubbed the 931, while right-hand drive models became known as the 932.

In 1980 Porsche released the 924 Carrera GT; it was clear that they intended to enter into competitions with their enhanced model. The 924 was developed into a race car by adding an intercooler to the engine and increasing compression to 8.5:1. Visually it differed to its predecessor through a number of styling changes. It had a polyurethane plastic front and rear-flared guards, in addition to a front spoiler. It no longer featured the NACA duct in the hood, but air intakes in the badge panel were still used and a top mounted air scoop was necessary for the intercooler. Both the 924 Carrera GT and the 924 Carrera GTS were offered as road-going cars in order to adhere to the homologation regulations, and generated 210 bhp and 245 bhp respectively.

The release of the 924 Carrera GTR race car signaled their ultimate development for the series. Featuring a highly modified 2.0-liter in-line four engine, the GTR could produce 375 bhp and 299 lb/ft of torque. Performance-wise, the GTR could achieve 0-60 in less than five seconds and had a top speed of 180 mph. Only 17 examples were built and Porsche enjoyed success with the car at the 24 Hours of Le Mans in 1980. They entered three cars, finishing in 6th, 12th, and 13th. Their most notable victory was at the 1982 24 Hours of Le Mans when the car

won the class on street tires.

In 1984 Volkswagen ceased production of the engine blocks used in the 2.0-liter 924, leading to Porsche reintroducing the 924 with a detuned version of the 944's 163 bhp 2.5-liter straight four, while keeping the 924's interior. Named the 924S, it could produce 150 bhp and could accelerate from 0-60 in 7.9 seconds. The sporty coupe could achieve a top speed of 145 mph, thanks to its lighter weight and more aerodynamic body than the standard 924 model.

928

The Porsche 928 was designed to be a replacement for the iconic 911, offering the power and handling of a contemporary sports car fused with the refined luxury and comfort that might appeal to a more executive market; the result was a honed Grand Tourer. As one of only six front-engined models, the 928 had the further distinction of being the first (and only) coupe with a front-mounted V8 engine.

Managing director Ernst Fuhrmann believed the 911 was approaching the end of its shelf life: it was experiencing a fall in sales, causing Ferry Porsche to explore designs for a new model. To set it apart from the pure sports car features of the 911, Fuhrmann wanted to create a range-topping model that would offer sports car

Produced	1977-1995
Engine Size	4474 cc
Cylinders	8
0-60 mph	8.1 secs
Top Speed	143 mph
Power Output	240 bhp
Transmission	Manual
Gears	5 speed
Length	175 in (4445 mm)
Width	72.3 in (1835 mm)
Height	51.9 in (1320 mm)
Weight	3196.7 lb (1450 kg)
Wheelbase	98.4 in (2500 mm)

(Specifications refer to 1977 Porsche 928)

performance with the styling and appearance of a luxury sedan.

The engine layout was tested in mid- and rear-mounted configurations before engineers finally settled on the front-mounted placement. This was largely due to issues with trying to fit the engine, transmission, catalytic converter, and exhaust into a confined area – something they had already managed with the rear-engined 911 but wanted to avoid for this particular model. There was much

debate over the powertrain for the 928; prototype units built with a 5.0-liter V8 could produce 300 bhp, which satisfied the Porsche engineers, but Ferdinand Piëch wanted to use a 5.0-liter V10 with 3.46-inch bore spacing based on Audi's five-cylinder engine. The final result was a 4.5-liter water-cooled V8 driving the rear wheels and Bosch K-Jetronic fuel injection system. In 1980, the fuel injection system was upgraded from mechanical to electronic, although

the power remained the same.

To aid the car's balance, Porsche utilized a transaxle, allowing 50/50 weight distribution. The innovative use of the Weissach axle, a rear-wheel steering system, provided increased stability when breaking during a turn and thus reduced the risk of over steer.

Designed by Wolfgang Möbius and styled by Tony Lapine, the 928 married bold wedged lines with opulent curves, seemingly having no apparent front or rear bumpers.

Instead they were integrated into the plastic nose and tail sections, allowing a clear-cut design and reducing drag. While the majority of the body was constructed from galvanized steel, aluminum was used as a lightweight material for the doors, front fenders, and hood.

The interior offered luxury coupled with a number of cleverly styled accessories. Leather seats and individual sun visors for both front and rear passengers ensured that occupants were comfortable

in transit. The steering wheel and instrument cluster adjusted together in order to maintain maximum instrument visibility at all times.

The use of innovative technologies and luxury styling for the 928 allowed it to claim the 1978 European Car of the Year, beating its main rivals BMW and Ford. This award was a first for a sports car, signaling just how advanced the model was.

It made its official debut at the 1977 Geneva Motor Show and

went on sale later that year with the 1978 model. However, sales for the 928 were slow despite numerous acclaim for its comfort, styling, and power. Although its original intention was to replace the 911, Fuhrmann's successor, Peter Schutz, felt that both cars should be sold alongside one another, each offering different attributes.

In 1980 Porsche introduced a front and rear spoiler to the refreshed model – the 928 S. Aesthetically it also demonstrated wider wheels and tires, but it was under the hood where changes had really taken place. An increased power output of 297 bhp was down to the revised 4.7-liter V8 that could boast a 0-60 performance of six seconds and a maximum speed of 155 mph.

Year on year Porsche continued to make subtle changes to the 928, improving its performance and making minor cosmetic changes. It was not until a decade after its first release that Porsche introduced a number of major changes with the release of the S4. Many of the major changes that it experienced were to the nose, tail, engine, and wheels. Externally the nose section was modified and a more significant rear spoiler was added. The engine capacity was increased to 4957 cc and the synchromesh gearbox was changed to the Borg Warmer design to offer improved drivability.

During its final year in production, in 1995, the 928 GTS, the last car of its line, boasted an astonishing 350 bhp capable of thrusting the car from 0-60 in 5.3 seconds and with a top speed of 171 mph.

The shape of the GTS combined the perfect blend of aggression with superior Porsche branding, resulting in the sportiest variant of the 928. Throughout its lifespan, the 928 developed a keen following of enthusiasts and remained in production for 18 years.

944

First introduced during 1982, the Porsche 944 was a sports coupe based on the earlier designs of the popular 924 model. With a redesigned front engine and body shape, the rear-wheel driven 944 would surpass its predecessor in many ways. Other than the fact that the 944 was generally faster, it was advertised as a more comfortable drive, with better handling and braking power than the 924 design. The 944 featured a straight four-cylinder engine that put out over 160 bhp with a top speed of 130 mph and 0-60 in 8.4 seconds. The aluminum alloy constructed coupe had a nearly completely balanced weight distribution of 50.7 per cent front and 49.3 per cent rear, making the 944 one of the easiest and predictable to handle (even at high speed) sports cars

that Porsche had built to date. In 1985 the 944 underwent its first changes to the standard model. The updated variant boasted a larger

Produced	1982-1991
Engine Size	2479 cc
Cylinders	4
0-60 mph	8.4 secs
Top Speed	130 mph
Power Output	163 bhp
Transmission	Manual
Gears	5 speed
Length	169.8 in (4313 mm)
Width	68.3 in (1735 mm)
Height	50.19 in (1275 mm)
Weight	2601 lb (1180 kg)
Wheelbase	94.4 in (2400 mm)

(Specifications refer to 1982 Porsche 944)

fuel tank, an upgraded alternator, a Porsche Hi-Fi system, optional heated seats, modification to the transaxle (to reduce noise and unwanted vibrations), among other cosmetic changes.

A total of 113,070 of the standard 944 model were manufactured between 1982 and 1989, with over 55,000 units having been exported

to the US. In 1990 the company's designers began working on a plan that was intended to become the 944 S3 model (the third redesign of the standard model), however, shortly into the developmental process, Porsche decided that due to the fact that so many parts were being changed and upgraded, they were more likely to benefit from creating a completely different car altogether. The 944 was subsequently replaced with the 968.

The 944 series of vehicles produced by Porsche featured a variety of models, including the 944 Turbo (1985), the 944 S (1987), the 944 S2, and the 944 Turbo Cabriolet. Between 1982 and 1991, 163,192 cars from the 944 series were built, making the 944 Porsches the most successful production vehicle in the company's history, right up until the introduction of the Boxster model in 1996.

959

Formally known as the Gruppe B (internally) when its design stage began in 1981, Porsche finally unveiled its 959 model at the Frankfurt Motor Show in 1986. Initially designed to be a Group B rally car, the 959 was modified to satisfy the FIA regulations to be considered a road-legal vehicle. The 959 featured a twin turbocharged six-cylinder 2.85-liter flat engine that impressed automotive fanatics with its impressive output of almost 450 bhp and top speed of 195 mph. The aluminum and Kevlar chassis design made the car more lightweight than most of its predecessors and competitors alike. Its aerodynamic design was also tailored for a more stable drive and increased handling, and when coupled with its four-wheel drive system (that could dynamically adapt the torque levels between the front and rear wheels), the lightweight supercar lived up to all of its expectations with its remarkable 0-60 in just 3.7 seconds and 370 lbs/ft of torque.

During production, the 959 was considered to be the most technically advanced road-legal sports car to have ever been manufactured and, in 2004, was

Produced	1986-1989
Engine Size	2847 cc
Cylinders	6
0-60 mph	3.7 secs
Top Speed	195 mph
Power Output	444 bhp
Transmission	Manual
Gears	6 speed
Length	167.7 in (4260 mm)
Width	72.4 in (1840 mm)
Height	50.39 in (1280 mm)
Weight	2535 lb (1450 kg)
Wheelbase	89.4 in (2272 mm)

(Specifications refer to 1986 Porsche 959)

POUNDSBRIDGE OAST

K330 RBK

voted number one by *Sports Car International* on their Top Sports Cars of the 1980s list. The engine management system, suspension tuning, and four-wheel drive technology set the standard for many Porsche models that followed, including the Carrera 4 and many subsequent variants of the 911 family. Inside the vehicle cabin were advanced features not fitted in its predecessors, such as the gauges that measured the amount of rear differential slip and how much power was being transmitted to the front axle.

The 959 was one of the first ever high-performance sports vehicles to have featured a four-wheel drive design, which after testing had convinced Porsche that all of their subsequent 911 models should also feature all-wheel drive as standard; this was initially introduced with the 933 model. Originally retailed at the cost of $225,000, just 337 units of the 959 were produced during its short production run between 1986 and 1989, when Porsche eventually ceased production in order to make way for the 911 GT1 Straßenversion.

968

The 968 was the final evolutionary stage of almost 20 years of vehicular and automotive technological development that began with the introduction of the Porsche 924. Produced in the Zuffenhausen Porsche factory, the 968 sports coupe was first introduced in 1992, when it superseded the 944 as the company's entry-level production car. Developed from the designs that were intended for the 944 S3 model, the 968 claimed the rights to Harm Lagaay's vastly upgraded design. The 968 was generally considered a more modern-shaped and aerodynamic design of its predecessor. Powered by an updated 16v straight-four engine, the 968 delivered 236 bhp, a top speed of 156 mph, and 0-60 in 6.1 seconds. The 968 featured the all-new VarioCam variable valve timing system, an upgraded electronic engine management system, a steel unibody construction, new intake

Produced	1992-1995
Engine Size	2990 cc
Cylinders	4
0-60 mph	6.1 secs
Top Speed	156 mph
Power Output	236 bhp
Transmission	Manual and tiptronic
Gears	6 speed and 4 speed
Length	170.1 in (4321 mm)
Width	68.3 in (1735 mm)
Height	50.19 in (1275mm)
Weight	3086.4 lb (1400 kg)
Wheelbase	94.48 in (2400 mm)

(Specifications refer to 1992 Porsche 968)

and exhaust fittings, among other various cosmetic modifications. Aesthetically the 968 featured visual resemblances to various other Porsche models, including the 924, 944, 928, and 959.

At the time of its manufacture the 968 had the second-largest four-cylinder engine ever to be placed into a production car, and both the six-speed manual transmission and four-speed tiptronic automatic transmission versions of the vehicle

provided a popular replacement to the 944. Historically, the 968 again has its place in Porsche's hall of fame because it was the last new front-engined model before the introduction of the Cayenne SUV, and also the last Porsche to feature a four-cylinder engine. Aside from the standard coupe, there were redesigns of the 968 throughout its short three-year production period, including the 968 Clubsport (1993), the 968 Turbo S (1993), and the 968 Turbo RS (1994). By the close of its production year in 1995, the 968 had been manufactured in small numbers, with only 12,776 cars having been produced (both standard coupe and cabriolet versions).

Boxster

Produced	1996 to present
Engine Size	2480 cc
Cylinders	6
0-60 mph	7.4 secs
Top Speed	158 mph
Power Output	204 bhp
Transmission	Manual or tiptronic
Gears	5 speed
Length	162.7 in (4133 mm)
Width	68.5 in (1740 mm)
Height	50.78 in (1290 mm)
Weight	2777.8 lb (1260 kg)
Wheelbase	95 in (2415 mm)

(Specifications refer to 1997 Porsche Boxster [generation II])

The Boxster is a two-door roadster that made its first appearance at the 1993 Detroit Motor Show in concept form. Its name derives from the word "**box**er" in reference to the boxer engine, and "speed**ster**" in reference to its body style. Upon its first outing it exuded a modern yet ageless appearance, evoking memories of 1950s glamour. Styled by Grant Larson and Stefan Stark, the Boxster was inspired by the design of the 356 Cabriolet, Speedster, and the 550 Spyder.

When released in 1996, the Boxster had lost some of its retro detailing, due to practicality and the pressure to compete with rivals BMW, with their Z3, and Mercedes, with the SLK. However, a market had opened up for an affordable first-class brand sports car and consultation with Toyota for parts enabled the release of a more readily available Porsche.

Unlike the 911, which had a rear-engined configuration, the Boxster's flat-six-cylinder engine is placed between the rear and front axles, providing a new center of gravity, excellent weight distribution, and neutral handling, while being incredibly agile; it was not as demanding as the 911, offering a more forgiving drive. Internally known as the 986, the Boxster shared much of the same design as the 996 that was later released in 1998.

The first generation Boxster featured a 2.5-liter engine that could produce 204 bhp, a respectable 0-60 performance of 7.4 seconds, and a top speed of 158 mph. Stylistically, this model has experienced very few cosmetic changes over the span of its lifetime and in true Porsche approach they have honed and refined the roadster to punch out maximum performance with more efficiency.

The present-day Boxster boasts lightweight largely aluminum

M44 SRS

body construction coupled with aerodynamic yet aesthetically appealing lines that have aided the development of a nimble sports car. The 2.7-liter engine produces 265 bhp, while the 3.4-liter engine of the Boxster S generates 315 bhp – both are mid-mounted, featuring a direct injection and VarioCam for a significant increase in power output and efficiency. In addition to the six-speed manual transmission, the Boxster is also available with the seven-speed PDK, incorporating both manual and automatic transmission. PDK enables the driver to change gear without interrupting the flow of power, while offering improved acceleration and short response times. Innovative technologies such as stop/start function, electrical system recuperation, and a coasting function all contribute to the reduction of CO_2 emissions and fuel consumption.

Cayenne

The Porsche Cayenne (Type 955) is a five-door mid-sized luxury crossover SUV that was first introduced in 2002; among the available models, some are more commonly known as the Type 955, Type 957, and Type 958. The front-engined four-wheel drive is said to be a luxurious exploration of everything that Porsche has to offer, in its sporty but comfortable design. The Cayenne's platform was designed by Porsche but developed alongside Volkswagen and their Touareg model, meaning that both share the same platform, body frame, and door design; however, it was Porsche's in-house adaptations and fine-tuning that put the Cayenne one step ahead of its competitors. Although the Cayenne S quickly replaced the first

generation of the Cayenne line, the first edition of the vehicle surprised critics and Porsche fanatics with its impressive output and incorporated modern design technologies. The 3.6-liter V6-powered Cayenne initially pushed out a surprising 300 bhp, a top speed of 143 mph, and 0-60 in just 7.5 seconds, exceeding the expectations of what was considered to be Porsche's version of the family car.

With regard to its exterior design, the Cayenne features some body styling that is reminiscent of older Porsches dating as far back as the 1960s, with its elongated hood previously featured on many models. Its bulbous hood, visibly drawn-in flanks, and pronounced wheel arches are of a distinguishable quality and are

unique to the Cayenne design. The Carrera GT was the inspiration for the contoured roof spoiler, which has again been integrated into the modern design of the Cayenne, with its tapered rear windscreen producing a distinctive rear view, typical of so many of its predecessors. On the inside of the car the list of modern accessories

Produced	2002 to present
Engine Size	3598 cc
Cylinders	6
0-60 mph	7.5 secs
Top Speed	143 mph
Power Output	300 bhp
Transmission	6 speed
Gears	Manual or tiptronic
Length	190.7 in (4846 mm)
Width	76.3 in (1939 mm)
Height	67.1 in (1705mm)
Weight	4564 lbs (2070 kg)
Wheelbase	114 in (2895 mm)

(Specifications refer to Porsche Cayenne [first generation])

continues, with its high-resolution TFT monitor displaying on-board computer information, as well as various warnings such as monitoring the change in tire pressure. A compass has also been installed within the five-instrument cluster, raised slightly from the dashboard – a common Porsche feature. Aside from the standard design of the Cayenne, Porsche also released the Cayenne S, Cayenne GTS, Cayenne Turbo, Cayenne Turbo S, Cayenne Diesel, Cayenne Transsyberia, and Cayenne GTS Porsche Design Edition 3.

Carrera GT

The Carrera GT is a high-performance, mid-engined sports car first introduced to the automotive market in 2004. The GT was originally designed as a racing vehicle (a Le Mans prototype in 1999) that had earlier been put on hold while the company focused their engineering and marketing efforts on the forthcoming Cayenne SUV model, which was being developed in partnership with Audi and Volkswagen. Upon the grand unveiling, Porsche boasted of a road-legal V10 supercar that posed great competition to its direct opposition. The Carrera GT demonstrated an incredible 605 bhp, top speed of 205 mph, and 0-60 in just 3.9 seconds. Its aerodynamic design featured large side inlets that allowed air to cool the powerful V10, and the automatically deployed rear wing (when the vehicle reaches a speed of 70 mph), which had previously been used in many of the 911 series design. The V10 engine was a design originally built behind closed doors by Porsche for the Footwork Formula One team back in 1992, but it was quickly shelved and later resurrected in 1999 for the concept model of the car.

Produced	2004-2007
Engine Size	5733 cc
Cylinders	10
0-60 mph	3.9 secs
Top Speed	205 mph
Power Output	605 bhp
Transmission	Manual
Gears	6 speed
Length	181.6 in (4613 mm)
Width	75.6 in (1921 mm)
Height	45.9 in (1166 mm)
Weight	3042 lb (1380 kg)
Wheelbase	107.4 in (2730 mm)

(Specifications refer to 2004 Porsche Carrera GT)

The construction of the bodywork was heavily designed around a carbon fiber monocoque and subframe, including the carbon-fiber-framed boot space that housed the V10. The impressive V10 engine meant that the GT required a radiator system that was almost five times the size of that as featured in a 911 Turbo. Porsche had fitted the Carrera with its newest invention: a carbon-fiber-reinforced silicon carbide ceramic composite braking system that gave an even further impressive aesthetic to the already head-turning bodywork of the vehicle. The Carrera GT was fitted with a Bose audio sound system, on-board navigation system, and a Beechwood-topped gear knob that paid homage to the original gear stick as featured in the early 917 Le Mans racing vehicles as standard. *Sports Car International* voted the Carrera GT number one in its Top Sports Cars of the 2000s, and later voted it number eight in the Top Sports Cars of All Time. Porsche had initially intended on the production of 1,500 units of the Carrera GT, however due to a change in airbag legislations in the United States they discontinued the model as they approached the manufacture of almost 1,300 vehicles.

Cayman

The Cayman S (Type 987120) is a rear mid-engined, rear-wheel driven sports coupe that has been developed as a derivative of the latter Boxster models. The "S" suffix was suggestive that there may have been a previous design of the vehicle that had not been produced for public sale; it was not until later in 2006 that the standard Cayman model was launched. Unveiled during the Frankfurt Motor Show in September of 2005, the Cayman S was given its name as an adaptation of the word Caiman, a reptile belonging to the alligator family; the reference is made to its somewhat reptilian-looking front end. The vehicle was designed with a 3.4-liter flat-six boxer engine that boasted an impressive 325 bhp, which combined with its six-speed manual transmission took the vehicle to a limit of 175 mph with 0-60 in just 5.0 seconds. The overall performance of the Cayman S has

been said to share similarities with that of the Porsche 911 Carrera forerunning sports vehicle and has caused speculation as to whether the Cayman S will outsell the Carrera over time due to its more affordable price tag.

The Cayman S is built with a rigid yet lightweight body construction, making for a

faster yet stable drive. For better handling and stability, the vehicle is fitted with the Porsche stability

Produced	2005 to present
Engine Size	3436 cc
Cylinders	6
0-60 mph	5.0 secs
Top Speed	175 mph
Power Output	325 bhp
Transmission	Manual or PDK
Gears	6 speed
Length	172.4 in (4380 mm)
Width	70.9 in (1801 mm)
Height	51 in (1295 mm)
Weight	3075 lbs (1395 kg)
Wheelbase	97.4 in (2475 mm)

(Specifications relate to Cayman S)

management system as standard, with the selective optional features including the Enhanced Porsche Active Suspension Management system and Porsche Torque Vectoring for increased rear agility. On the outside, the Cayman S features well-sculpted lines and defined edges: a true representation of Porsche's development in their aesthetic evolution design work. The large dynamic air intakes (that cool both the engine and the braking systems) give the car its classic Porsche look, supported by the redesigned automatically deployed rear wing when the vehicle reaches a speed of 74 mph; the spoiler has been given a larger aerodynamic surface to ensure less lift and more traction with the ground below. The inside of the Cayman S continues to impress, with its spacious but sporty interior design. Many smaller features have been developed from Porsche's racing models and housed within the Cayman to provide a sportier drive with a race feeling; the ascending center console and repositioned gear lever (that now sits close to the steering wheel) are just two of these features. This uncompromising sports car is certainly destined to give other leading Porsche models a run for their money.

Panamera

The Panamera (internally known as the Type 970) was given its name after the well-known Carrera Panamericana race: a border-to-border open road race that stretched across the country of Mexico. First unveiled in 2009, the production model of the Panamera luxury four-door GT was introduced during the 13th Shanghai International Automobile show in China, much to the disbelief of Porsche fanatics who scorned the vehicle and its maker for not staying true to their sporty heritage. Little did they know that the Panamera actually exceeded many of its expectations as an SUV, with its sporty features and performance ratings. The Type 970 was the realization of an earlier model called the 989 concept that was designed and then shelved back in 1998. The front-engined Panamera turbo-diesel wowed critics with its six-cylinder 3.6-liter engine, which proclaimed an impressive 310 bhp, a top speed

of 160 mph, and 0-60 in just 6.3 seconds. The lightweight V6 engine provided the car with a more balanced weight distribution for better handling.

Produced	2009 to present
Engine Size	3605 cc
Cylinders	6
0-60 mph	6.3 secs
Top Speed	160 mph
Power Output	310 bhp
Transmission	Dual clutch (PDK)
Gears	7-speed
Length	197.5 in (5015 mm)
Width	76 in (1931 mm)
Height	55.83 in (1418 mm)
Weight	3902 lbs (1770 kg)
Wheelbase	115 in (2920 mm)

(Specifications refer to 2009 Porsche Panamera)

Unlike many of its two-door predecessors, the Panamera has a luxurious interior that features many modern technological accessories, including heated front seats, partial leather seat covering, electrically adjusted front seat height and backrest angle adjustment, air conditioning, automatic climate control, park assist, cruise control, and particle/pollen filter to name but a few. With regard to its exterior design features

the Panamera is reminiscent of many other Porsche designs, with its elongated front intake vents (that help to cool the engine and braking systems), tapering rear roof line, and muscular body shape. Although the initial launch of the Panamera was considered to be a risk, the car has gone on to be praised as the perfect balance between a sedan and a sports car and has won various comparative tests against other competitive four-door performance vehicles (notably the Maserati Quattroporte and the Aston Martin Rapide). Since 2009 Porsche have released various versions of the car, including the Panamera, Panamera 4, Panamera Diesel, Panamera S, Panamera 4S, Panamera GTS, Panamera S Hybrid, Panamera Turbo, and Panamera Turbo S, which are still globally popular and selling in the present day.

918 Spyder

Originally unveiled at the 2010 80th anniversary Geneva Motor Show, although production didn't begin until three years later, the Porsche 918 Spyder is a mid-engined plug-in hybrid sports car with a lot to boast about. Designed by Michael Mauer, the 918 Spyder is a limited-edition model that Porsche plan to distribute throughout 2014. With the intention of producing 918 units of the road version of the vehicle, the 918 is able to boast some incredible specifications. The 918 produces 940 lb/ft of torque, with its 4.6-liter V8 that pushes out an incredible top speed of 214 mph, with a 0-60 sprint in just

2.6 seconds. The total power output of the 918 is an impressive 887 bhp, which combines the power of the engine (608 bhp) and two electrical motors that directly drive the front and rear axles (154 bhp rear and 125 bhp front). The supercar offers a variation of different driving modes: E-drive (when the car runs purely from electrical battery power) and three hybrid modes (hybrid, sport, and race). In E-drive mode, the car uses only the electronic motors that power the front and rear axles and can drive the car for a range of up to 18 miles, with a top speed of 93 mph. The energy storage battery is a liquid-cooled lithium-ion battery

that utilizes regenerative braking as a charging feature alongside the plug-in charging port.

The 918 is constructed using a carbon fiber reinforced plastic monocoque, a contributing factor to the vehicle's aerodynamic

Produced	2013 to present
Engine Size	4593 cc
Cylinders	8
0-60 mph	2.6 secs
Top Speed	214 mph
Power Output	887 bhp
Transmission	Dual-clutch
Gears	7 speed
Length	182.7 in (4643 mm)
Width	76.3 in (1940 mm)
Height	45.9 in (1167 mm)
Weight	3747.8 lb (1700 kg)
Wheelbase	107.4 in (2730 mm)

(Specifications refer to 2013 Porsche 918 Spyder)

performance. The proposed retail price of the 918 Spyder is a staggering $845,000, meaning that the short run of these vehicles is intended for the elite end of the market. In 2012 a racing version of the 918 – named the 918 RSR – was introduced during the North American International Auto Show. In September 2013 a 918, fitted with the optional Weissach package, secured a new Nürburgring lap time of 6:57 on its 12.8-mile course, beating the previous record by a staggering 14 seconds, making the 918 the first production road-legal vehicle to have ever beaten the seven-minute marker. The popularity of the 918 Spyder since its release has seen the car feature in many modern video games, such as *Need For Speed: Hot Pursuit, Real Racing 3,* and *Shift 2: Unleashed.*

Macan

Manufactured by Porsche AG, the Macan (internally known as the Type 95B) is a further development into the company's compact crossover sport SUV series of vehicles, alongside the Panamera and the Cayenne. Originally the Macan was first introduced in 2010 during its concept stages, where it was initially identified under the working title of the name "Cajun," derived from the concept that the vehicle was being developed as the Cayenne Junior. It was not until 2012 that Porsche finally announced the vehicle's name as the Macan, deriving from the Indonesian word for "Tiger." The Macan featured at two separate formal launch events, the 2013 Los Angeles Auto Show and the 2013 Tokyo Auto Show, and shortly after, in 2014, the formal production and manufacture of the car began in Europe. Although the Macan is generally considered to be a somewhat inferior model to the Cayenne, the Macan actually poses a sportier drive and feel due to the seven-speed dual clutch PDK transmission, which provides the car with a more responsive gearshift transition.

Marketed as a sports car with five doors and five seats, the intention of this impressive compact SUV is clear. With its 3.0-liter V6 engine, capable of producing 340 bhp, it's

Produced	2014 to present
Engine Size	2997 cc
Cylinders	6
0-60 mph	5.4 secs
Top Speed	157 mph
Power Output	340 bhp
Transmission	Dual clutch (PDK)
Gears	7 speed
Length	184.3 in (4681 mm)
Width	75.7 in (1923 mm)
Height	64 in (1624 mm)
Weight	4277 lbs (1940 kg)
Wheelbase	110.5 in (2807 mm)

(Specifications refer to Porsche Macan S)

no wonder that Porsche wanted to advertise this vehicle in the right manner to demonstrate its true potential. With a top speed of 157 mph and 0-60 in a mere 5.4 seconds, the Macan really is a sportier model than the Cayenne standard edition. The Macan is considered to be the sister car to the Audi Q5, as Porsche admits that one third of its construction platform is indeed shared with Audi; the similarities lay within the fact that the Macan has a longitudinally mounted engine that sits slightly ahead of the front axle and that some of the internal framework is identical to that of its competitor. Alongside the

technical features that lie beneath the hood, the Macan again boasts of many luxury interior accessories too, such as the multifunctional steering wheel, the all-wheel drive traction management system, air suspension, powerful bi-xenon

headlights, and a Burmester surround sound audio system to name a few. There are currently three varying models available in the Macan range: the Macan S, the Macan Turbo, and the Macan S Diesel.

Competitive Spirit

Over the past six decades Porsche has become the most successful name in motorsport, enjoying numerous victories in endurance racing, hillclimb events, rallying, and Formula One (with McLaren). They have had a monumental impact, with more than 28,000 victories, including a record 16 constructor wins in the 24 Hours of Le Mans, 18 outright victories at the Daytona 24-Hour, 11 wins at the Targa Florio, and a further 17 victories at the 12 Hours of Sebring, proving that they have become endurance racing masters.

The first Le Mans success for Porsche was a class win in 1951 with their 1.1-liter 356, and in 1970 they achieved their first overall win with a 917 5.0-liter, 12-cylinder coupe. However, it was during the 1980s that Porsche experienced repeated success, winning 24 Hours of Le Mans for seven consecutive years from 1981.

More recently Audi have dominated Le Mans, but their string of success could be due to end, with Porsche's announcement to return. During their 16-year absence Porsche have been developing and perfecting a car to mark their return to the highest level of sports car racing. The result: the 919 Hybrid, unveiled at the 2014 Geneva Motor Show. The 919 Hybrid has been constructed especially for Le Mans and the World Endurance Championships and is the first sports prototype built since the RS Spyder. Porsche spent 2,000 hours of wind tunnel testing to fine-tune the aerodynamic body. It is powered by a turbocharged 2.0-liter V4 engine and equipped with two energy recuperation systems: KERS, which recovers kinetic energy from the brakes on the front axle, and

■ ABOVE: The Porsche 919 Hybrid during testing.
■ OPPOSITE: The Porsche 956 T driven by Jacky Ickx and Derek Bell wins the 1982 24 Hours of Le Mans car race.

AER (which stands for Abgasen energierueckgewinnung) – a system that recovers energy from exhaust gases.

In 1960 Porsche experienced their first overall win at 12 Hours of Sebring, and have gone on to achieve 16 further overall wins as well as 47 class wins with 911, 917, 935, and 962 models.

The American Le Mans Series introduced in 1999 has also offered Porsche the opportunity to scoop more titles including most class wins, longest winning streak, and most pole positions. The 911 GT3 R, introduced at the start of the 1999 racing season, went on to become one of the most successful sports cars in GT history.

Hillclimbing is not widely publicized outside of Europe, although it remains popular in Germany, and for many years

Porsche dominated the sport. The factory team can boast 20 European hillclimb championship titles in addition to the numerous second and third positions and individual event wins. Unmodified 550 Spyders were used until 1962, when Ferrari beat them to first place with the Dino 196SP, causing Porsche to focus on specifically developing cars for this event. Their ambition and drive to succeed led them to the creation of the 906 – a tube-framed topless model, weighing only 1100 lbs (500 kg). The body received extensive wind tunnel testing in order to improve its aerodynamics. Porsche had built a match for Ferrari and went on to dominate the hillclimb events. In 1969 Porsche decided to depart from hillclimbing in order to focus on sports car racing, although privateers continued to race numerous Porsche models.

Rallying and off-road racing are an important part of Porsche's sporting heritage. They enjoyed numerous successes in rallying with long-distance desert tracks such as Paris-Dakar, snow rallying in Scandinavia, and road-based races such as the Monte Carlo dash.

In 1984 Porsche developed the 953, a specially modified variant of the 911 featuring a manually controlled four-wheel drive system, designed specifically to compete in the Paris-Dakar Rally. Three 953s were entered with one scooping first place driven by René Metge and Dominique Lemoyne. Despite the success it achieved the model was short-lived and was soon replaced by the highly successful 959.

Porsche have not experienced major successes in Formula One like their rivals Ferrari, BMW, and Mercedes. Their only constructor win in Formula One was in 1962 with US driver Dan Gurney.

However, they have contributed to Formula One vehicles as an engine supplier.

In the 21st century Porsche has continued to be a powerful competitor in sports car racing and they remain the world's largest race car manufacturer. In 2006 they built 195 race cars for a variety of international sports events. This number increased to a staggering 275 dedicated race cars including RS Spyder LMP2s, 911 GT3-RSRs, and 911 GT3s making up the majority.

The Porsche racing pedigree is constantly reflected in the design and performance of their road cars. It is no secret that their number one goal is to develop race cars and prototypes that can aid the development of production vehicles in addition to seeking racing success.

■ **LEFT:** This Porsche 953 won the Paris-Dakar race in 1984. It's a highly modified all-wheel drive Porsche 911.

■ **OPPOSITE INSET:** A Porsche 997 GT3 Cup R in a spectacular jump.

■ **BELOW:** Cornering in a Porsche 911 GT3 R.

Prototypes and the Future

Porsche have paved their way throughout history to become the leading sports car manufacturer, using technology and drivability in production vehicles that derives from race car models as their focus. For more than 60 years the company have continued to develop and explore innovative technological advancements as a means of securing the number one spot as the world's leading sports car creator. Historically, the 911 marked numerous technological advancements including the introduction of four-wheel drive, turbocharging, tiptronic transmission, and VarioCam.

Through all of the unique engineering beneath the hood, within their interior developments and exterior aerodynamic shaping, Porsche have approached 2014 with an entirely new concept for their production vehicles – the plug-in hybrid. Although the Panamera was the first in the Porsche production car range to have featured the plug-in hybrid technology, the prestigious manufacturer has

refined its technology into its most recent 918 Spyder model. The Porsche 918 is an important car as, not only does it secure the future of Porsche, it heralds the direction for all sports car manufacturers.

It blends tradition with innovation and truly marks a turning point for the company through use of an exclusively designed V8 engine, PDK transmission, and top-mounted exhaust pipes deriving from racetrack models. Electric motors are positioned in front of the rear axle and behind the

■ **OPPOSITE ABOVE:** A Porsche 911 brochure.

■ **OPPOSITE BELOW:** The Porsche Panamera (Type 970), with hybrid engine, on display at the 81st International Motor Show in Geneva.

■ **BELOW:** A Porsche 918 Spyder.

front axle, providing an additional power source to the combustion engine and generating an additional mechanical power output of 286 bhp. The high-performance hybrid battery recharges while the car is in motion through the regenerative braking system. Engineers have also developed active aerodynamics (PAA) to reduce drag and increase downforce through the use of the three-stage extendable rear-wing and active cooling air-flaps in the front air intakes.

Inspired by racing technology once again, Porsche have used ceramic composite brakes that are lighter than standard discs to enhance performance and fuel economy. To top it off the 918 Spyder is more economical and has lower emissions than a Toyota Prius, proving that it really is the key to "greener" supercars of the future.

Innovation continues in the cockpit, with a multifunction steering wheel that reinforces one of the motorsport principles that a driver's hands should never

leave the steering wheel, while the center console offers fast navigation to creature comforts such as air conditioning, car settings, and the Porsche Communication Management (for personal device connectivity) – all on a gesture recognition touch screen surface.

Heading into the future, Porsche are destined to produce "greener" and even more elaborate sports cars in addition to their already rich automotive history. Rumor has it that the manufacturer is making final preparations for its launch of the Porsche 960 – a mid-engined 600+bhp sports car, said to be the fusion of the 911 Turbo and the 918 Spyder in terms of power, performance, and luxury.

Aesthetically the 960 is said to resemble the look of the Cayman, but is more powerful, slightly larger, and much more expensive. It is said that the four-wheel drive supercar will feature a seven-speed dual clutch transmission and 3.9-liter engine to assist with its targeted 0-60 sprint of just 2.5 seconds.

■ **BELOW: Porsche employees work on a Porsche 918 Spyder at the Porsche plant in Stuttgart-Zuffenhausen, Germany. The car's clever extendable rear wing is on show.**